We Are His People and the Sheep of His Pasture

by Barbara Jackson Johnson

DORRANCE
PUBLISHING CO
EST. 1920
PITTSBURGH, PENNSYLVANIA 15238

Dorrance Publishing Co
585 Alpha Drive
Suite 103
Pittsburgh, PA 15238
Visit our website at *www.dorrancebookstore.com*

ISBN: 979-8-89127-946-9
eISBN: 979-8-89127-444-0

We Are His People and the Sheep of His Pasture

I dedicate this book to:
My God in heaven
My family and friends

PSALM 100:3

KNOW YE THAT THE LORD HE IS GOD: IT IS HE THAT HAVE
MADE US, AND NOT WE OURSELVES; WE ARE HIS PEOPLE,
AND THE SHEEP OF HIS PASTURE.

A TIME TO BE BORN, A TIME TO FLY AWAY

A child named Lisa is born unto her parents, molded
with a spirit sent from above:
With a message that says: this is my gift to you,
to nourish and to love.

Teach her to keep my commandments, and guide
her in the righteous way.
But you must always remember that I must come
back to reclaim her one day.

Lisa grows up, gets an education, and gets married
to her choice of mate.
The couple experience many trials as they raise their
children to be obedient, and not to hate.

The creator comes back at the least unexpected hour to reclaim
Lisa and to take her away.
Her parents Joshua and Cora, if they were living, would say: Heavenly Father, we knew you
were coming back,
but, oh how we wish it were a later day.

Her husband Robert says: You were the other half that made
me complete.
Sometimes I even took it for granted that you would be
mine for keeps.

Her children, her boys, her sons Robert and Christian say: Mother,
we will never find anyone to take your precious place.
We will miss you dearly, and it's going to be so hard not being able
to see your face.

Her sisters, brothers, family, and friends say: We wish you could have stayed longer,
but God knows best:
May you go where the chilly winds don't blow to get your eternal rest.

The deceased child Lisa says to all: I'm not dead! My body was tired and
worn, so I spread my wings, and I flew away.
Let my spirit continue to live on in you, and I will meet you all on the
other side one sweet day.

WHERE DO I GO FROM HERE

At an early age I was taught to believe; I was taught to have faith in only you.

I thank those who helped to establish my foundation, which is built on your promises that are true.

Over the years my ups and downs had begun to level off and the problems seemed to be few.

Then comes a major storm which has shattered my world, leaving me feeling lost, hopeless, knowing not what to do.

I am on the brink of sinking, my soul cries out to you, pleading for you to send me a life-line…

Praying for you to ease my heartaches and pains, and to bring peace to my wandering mind:

WANDERING:

I ask: Why did this happen to me, will my life ever be the same…

My creator replies: No, my child, a major storm brings about a major change…

I ask: I now truly know that life is uncertain, but…where do I go from here…

*My creator replies: Keep standing on my promises, keep the faith, and always remember: **I am forever near.***

MY TRAVELING DAYS HERE IS ALL DONE

Life here is a journey. For some it is a long one and for others it is a very short time.

Travel your journey with care. Enjoy your life to the fullest, but always keep your mission on your mind.

Try to make a difference for God by showing your love; do not let your living here be all about just "you."

This place is not your home. Always remember we are only travelers just passing through.

There were many hills that I had to climb, and so many dark valleys that I had to travel through.

And, yes, I did worry even though the Lord told me: I will never leave, never will I forsake you.

I did get a chance to plant beautiful flowers which are my niece, my family, and my friends.

Life is uncertain, but death is sure, and I knew that one day my journey would come to an end.

I don't know for sure where my next destination stop will be, but for here I feel that my victory has been won!

I got my ticket in my hand, I say farewell to you all, because you see, my TRAVELING days here are all done.

LOOKING THROUGH THE WINDOWS OF A LIFETIME...

Looking through the windows of a lifetime I see a child named Lucious
      running, playing, and getting into many fights.
So young, so innocent, so fearless, always trying
      to climb the highest heights.

Lucious is raised by his parents, with strict discipline, and
      plenty of love.
He attends church and reads the Holy Bible to learn
      about his God above.

Lucious attends school, becomes an adult, sets goals, and has
      dreams of a life that he wants to live.
All the while deep down inside he knows there is service
      for his God that he also must give.

When Lucious's departure time arrived, his goals and his dreams passed
      before his eyes, never to be achieved.
He looked up above and said: I offer no excuses, I tell no lies, I only
      want you Lord to have mercy on me.

I only blame myself for my shortcomings, and now I do realize that I can't
      change things from what they be.
I only ask that you judge me O Lord according to my righteousness,
      and according to mine integrity that is in me.

The Holy Spirit answered Luscious and said: For by grace are ye saved through
      Faith...
It is the gift of God above.

Grace, mercy, and peace be with you, from God the Father, and from
      the Lord Jesus Christ...

In truth, and in love.

AN INCREDIBLE HONOR TO BE USED BY GOD

This journey called LIFE is a road filled with many potholes, bumps, and
     unseen dangers at hand.
You see, I am just one of God's soldiers traveling through trying to
     get to the Promised Land.

God is a god of truth, and he never promised me my days would always
     be filled with sunshine, and never rain.
He never promised me that this fleshly body of mine would
     never experience pain.

Even though I get so tired, even though sometimes I get weak, I know
     my purpose is in the service that I give.
You see, I realized a long time ago when I accepted him in my heart that
     I was created for him.

My life belongs to him, my joy is in him, and that is why I can't do the
     things that I used to do.
Each day I give thanks, look up, and say: Lord help me to finish my
     course, and make it back home to you.

So, when the travels of this life gets rough, I slip away, find me a
     quiet place, and to him I pour out my heart.
He gives me strength to travel on, and my soul rejoices because it is
     "an incredible honor to be used by God."

A City for Me…

My time here on this side was just like a glory to my God come true…
An inheritance, incorruptible and undefiled reserved in heaven just for me.
I had my share of the good times here, and I had my share of the many rainy days too.
I learned to trust God, to believe in God. He will love you, he will cherish you, and he will always see you through…

Jesus says to us, I am the way, the truth, and the life: no man cometh unto the Father but by me.
I am asleep now waiting on the Lord to take me to that beautiful city just for me to see.
He that cometh to God must "believe that he is, and he will reward them that honestly seek him with love."
I am waiting for a city, which has a foundation, whose builder and maker is our Lord God above.

I am asleep now waiting on the Lord to take me to that beautiful city just for me to see.
God is not ashamed to be called our God: for he hath prepared a city of love just for me…

SPINNING WHEELS, GOING NOWHERE

During those last few days, I had a lot of time on my hands, and God opened my eyes to things that I needed to see.
I had come to realize that a lot of changes had to be made, and I even made a promise to take better care of me.

As I lay there meditating, I prayed for the Lord to heal my body and to help me get back on my feet.
You see, I was still worrying about all the works undone that I needed to complete.

As I lay there praying and thinking, I begin to notice some unfamiliar changes begin to take place.
A strange calmness came over my body, and one by one I could feel each of my worries begin to fade.

Suddenly, the problems didn't seem to matter anymore, and I begin to experience a complete peace.
And as my spirit slowly absorbed these incredible feelings, I knew without a doubt what was happening to me.

The entire journey of my life slowly scrolled out before my face: I saw the good, I saw the bad, and I saw a lot of valuable time that I did waste.

I then realized that I was on the last page of the last chapter, and there was nothing in my life that I could reach back and change.
All I could do is look up and say: Lord, have mercy, as the angel called my name.

The angel said: I come to fetch thee: do you have any final requests, do you have any messages for me to relay?
I humbly replied yes, to my family and friends I have these words to say:

TIME belongs to God, inventory your life, and ask God to fill your heart with love and care.
Believe in God, get to know God, spend more time with him because living your life without him is just like:
Spinning your wheels, and going nowhere…

Keep a Smile on Your Face… and a Song in Your Heart

All I could say is, Father, here am I when my departure time arrived,
    and God called my name the other day.
You see, the day that I was born into this world
    I was also appointed a time to end my stay.

And as I passed from this world, the entire journey of my life
    slowly scrolled out before my face.
I saw all the good, I saw all the bad, and I saw
    a lot of valuable time that I did waste.

To my family, to my friends, my enemies, and everyone else,
    God sends a message for all to behold:
TIME is more valuable than any money.
    TIME carries more weight than any silver or gold.

So not knowing when **OUR** appointed time will come,
    we must redeem our time wisely each day.
We must love each other, we must forgive each other,
    and offer hope and encouragement to each other in every way.

Yesterday is gone, tomorrow may never come, so we must
    take advantage of **TODAY** to do our part.
If we pray for strength and guidance from God above, he will help us keep a smile on our face,
    and a song in our heart.

YOUR LOVING TOUCH…(A TRIBUTE TO A LOVED ONE)

God crowned your body with his love and favor from the top of your head to the bottom of your feet,
        giving you a command to share his love with family,
friends, and everyone that you do meet.

Your eyes, mirrors of the love in your heart which expresses your faith in your God that you trust so much,
        allows you to extend to everyone love, kindness, a
beautiful smile: *your loving touch*.

A long journey traveled, many miles walked, with so many changes that you had to undertake.
        But your knowledge and wisdom taught us: God's
love is the bridge to carry us over to reach a better day.

Through your inspiration, and your encouraging words you have blessed us with: *your loving touch*.
        The legacy of your love will carry on through many
generations because we love you so much.

LAYING DOWN BY THE STILL WATERS

(Taking a rest till judgement day)

My journey got rough sometimes, filled with many heartaches, worries, sicknesses, and lots of pain.
But, as I look back overall, I can see nothing but the love of God in everything.

When I realized that it was my time to go, I looked up above and I said: O Lord, I do lift up my soul unto thee.
My angel hugged me and embraced me and said: You fought a good fight; I come to set you free.

Leaving was so hard: I could feel the love of God drawing me closer and closer to himself to bind.
I could hear him say, I know you are torn because of your ties to all the loved ones you leave behind.

I could feel the love of my family. I could hear all the sincere prayers they sent up to God for me to stay.
But I am all right now. I am at peace for God has lain me down by the still waters to take a rest until my judgement day.

On those sad, sad days ahead when the pain of grief hurt you so bad and it cut you so very deep,
close your eyes, relax your mind, look up toward heaven, and remember that I am not dead, I only fell asleep.

To my family and friends: keep yourselves in the love of God; acknowledge him
In all things and he shall direct thy pathways.
I am all right now. I am okay. I am just laying down by these still waters, taking a rest until my judgement day.

"IN MY GRANDMOTHER'S EYES"

Grandmother, we give thanks to God above for the
 blessings of having you still around in our lives.
We know that you get tired, and we know that you get weak
 as you try to finish out your miles.

In my grandmother's eyes we see pride and joy when
 another generation has entered this world.
We can feel the love of your powerful prayers that you send
 to your God above.

You see, a grandmother knows that our journey will be full of
 many pitfalls and fiery darts.
That is why she always encourages us to love and forgive each other,
 and to always keep God in our hearts.

In my grandmother's eyes we see tears of sadness when we
 stumble and wrong decisions we make.
We still feel the love in her heart as she scolds us and encourage us
 to seek God to keep from making the same mistakes.

In my grandmother's eyes we can see all the love in her heart
 that she feels for all her kin.
Grandmother, the legacy of your love will live on through
 our family until the very end.

WHEN YOU WALK WITH GOD

You Will Never Walk Alone…

We knew that you were tired from all your sufferings, and we knew that your body was weak.
Still, we wanted to have you for just a little while longer, to love, and to keep.

Your passing feels like a bad dream, and all we want to do is just wake up from this sleep.
But then we realize that your angel came and carried you, and from all your crosses he has set you free.

Not being able to visit you, not being able to see you is almost too much for our hearts to bear.
We cry a river of tears, knowing that when we stop by you are no longer there.

In spite of our shortcomings, in spite of our mistakes, you showered us with unconditional love.
And because of the love that you have instilled in us we will carry on…through the power of our God above.

In the midst of your tears when the sting of my death is cutting you so very deep:
Just close your eyes and imagine me sitting by the riverside, asking God to help you with your grief.

I didn't want to leave you, and I hesitated as my angel hugged me and said: Come, I take you to a beautiful place.
Imagine me sitting on that beautiful shore with the sun gently warming my face.

On those lonely days ahead when you are sad from missing me and realizing that I am really gone:
Please allow God's love to heal you, and always remember: **when you walk with God, you will never walk alone**.

THE COMMON LINK

A common link was discovered, so a decision was made
      get married.
The couple was eager and excited, not knowing the weight
      that their decision carried.

There were doubts, the bride and groom was scared, because
      this was something new for them both.
But the common link reassured them that in this new experience
      they could find much happiness and growth.

Marriage is a sacred commitment that must be regarded
      as pure gold.
For where your treasure is, there the love in your heart
      will behold.

A marriage blessed and sanctified by God's love is
      such a great wonder.
Where therefore what God hath joined together let not
      man put asunder.

The common link may get overshadowed by difficulties with the
      children or financial loss.
But the common link must be nourished and polished to
      keep it shiny and glossy.

The common link will always help a marriage overcome
      any bad situation that it may be in:
The common link pulls two people together and lets them
      realize that they are each other's best friend.

The common link shared by two will always need
      encouragement, strength, and guidance from above.
The common link will keep two people together in spite of all
      their trial because that common link is…**LOVE**

A MOTHER'S PRAYER

A child is a gift bestowed upon his parents,
　　　　a blessing sent from God above.
Upon arrival come the charge to raise it
　　　　with strict discipline and plenty of love.

He is taught to keep God's commandments,
　　　　he is guided in all the right ways.
But then the child grows up, becomes influenced by others,
　　　　the child then begins to go astray.

He goes out on his own and decides to start living his life
　　　　according to his own will.
He chooses negative friends, negative habits,
　　　　and a negative way to live.

When her child is in trouble and evil forces
　　　　has trapped him in their snares:
A mother will fall down on her knees and ask the Lord
　　　　to please receive her prayer.

She looks up above and says: Father, I've had financial loss,
　　　　and loss of many nights sleep.
I've done all that I can, so Father,
　　　　to you this child I now release…

I can't give him the strength to resist
　　　　all the temptations he's going through.
I can only pray that he will get on the right pathway
　　　　and find his way back home to you.

You see, with tears on her face,
　　　　she's praying from the very depths of her heart.
She's asking her Lord to reach down, pick her child up,
　　　　and give him a brand-new start.

There are so many children lost in the world,
　　　　thinking that no one really cares.
But Jesus has his angels watching over them
　　　　because he is listening to…
　　　　　　and receiving…**A Mother's Prayer**.

EVERYTHING IS GOING TO BE
ALL RIGHT AFTER AWHILE

Long time ago God designed the map for this journey that
we all are traveling upon.
And we must remember that the race is not always to the swift,
nor the battle to the strong.

On this journey we will have trials and there will be lots of pain
and suffering in our lives.
God will never forsake us; he will come at the needed hour to
reassure us that *everything is going to be all right after awhile*.

We know that God's love for us is pure because of what he allowed his
only begotten son Jesus to be put through.
And he left instructions here for us to keep his commandments, and to
love ye one another as I have loved you.

Sometimes it seems like we have to suffer for so long, sometimes
it even seems like God is nowhere to be found.
But you see, God is God all by himself; he does things in his own way,
and in his own time.

When the storms of life rage all around us and we feel like we just
can't make that last mile,
God will send an angel of mercy to comfort us, and to let us know that
"Everything is going to be all right after awhile."

GOOD SENSE

Life is all about choices: if we choose God, everything that we need, to us he will give.
It all starts with the ways of our thinking: if we change the way we think, we just might be able to change the way we live.

We have a good spirit, we have a bad spirit, and one of them determines whether it's a good sense, or bad sense that we will use. **GOD** is that good spirit, and if we obey his voice, he will show us the things that we need to do.

We can't keep living in this world not caring about each other, not caring about ourselves, and living like time is ours to waste.
TIME belongs to God; when he calls our name and we must lay down and die, our souls will need a resting place.

We need to stand for something, stop existing for nothing, wandering around taking up living space.
If we choose God he will teach us how to use our **GOOD SENSE** to change our ways.

Lisa H Smith (1967–2019)   A TIME TO BE BORN, A TIME TO FLY AWAY

Ronnie J Jackson (1957–2015)   WHERE DO I GO FROM HERE

Lula Reid (1915–2015)   MY SERVING DAYS HERE ARE ALL DONE

Lucious Ambler Jr. (1950–2018)   LOOKING THROUGH THE WINDOWS OF A LIFETIME

Kelson Brooks (1950–2017)   AN INCREDIBLE HONOR TO BE USED BY GOD

Kelley Dawsey Jr (1931–2021)   A CITY FOR ME…

Kenneth Scott (1958–2014)   SPINNING WHEELS, GOING NOWHERE

Andrew Jones (1961–2016)   KEEP A SMILE ON YOUR FACE…AND A SONG IN YOUR HEART

Ruby Jackson (1926–2022)   YOUR LOVING TOUCH…(A TRIBUTE TO A LOVED ONE)

Annie R Williams (1941–2018)   LAYING DOWN BY THE STILL WATERS…(Taking a rest till judgement day)

Fannie Wiley (1915–2015)   IN MY GRANDMOTHER'S EYES

Bessie Johnson (1932–2013)   WHEN YOU WALK WITH GOD…You Will Never Walk Along

Samuel Robinson (1944–2006)   THE COMMON LINK
Ethel Robinson (*)

Julia Mae Jackson (*)   A MOTHER'S PRAYER

Rhonda Little (*) (1971-2024)   EVERYTHING IS GOING TO BE ALRIGHT AFTER A WHILE
Eric Little (*)

David Walton (1936–2005)   GOOD SENSE
Annie P Turner (1928–2003)